IMAGES
*of America*

# OVERLAND PARK

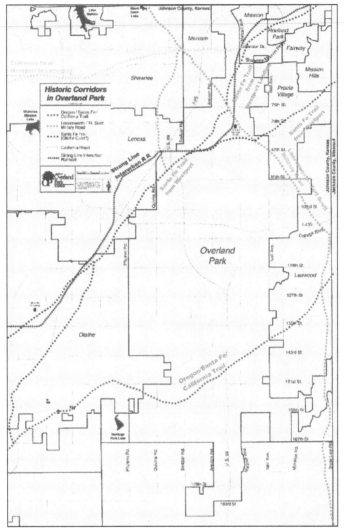

**Historic Corridors in Overland Park**

Legend:
- Oregon / Santa Fe / California Trail
- Leavenworth / Ft. Scott Military Road
- Santa Fe Trail (Olathe Cutoff)
- California Road
- Strang Line Interurban Railroad

This map indicates where the Westport Route of the Santa Fe Trail crossed what is now the old downtown of Overland Park. Authorities state that in a six-month period in 1865, some 5,197 men, 6,452 mules, 38,281 oxen, and 4,472 wagons traversed the trail. In 1866, over 5,000 wagons carried $40 million worth of goods. Settlers poured into the Kansas Territory, exploding its population from 8,600 in 1855 to 143,000 by 1861. Another route through Kansas, also on the map, crossed through what would become Overland Park as well. It was more southerly and combined with the Oregon and California Trails crossing the Military Road, which would become Metcalf Avenue, a current major north-south traffic artery in the city. For many years, until housing and business developments obliterated them, the swales left by the heavily laden wagons could still be seen. (Courtesy Overland Park Historical Society.)

ON THE COVER: Popular entertainment in early Overland Park made it necessary to use open-air trailers to transport multiple loads of people from the city on the Strang interurban line to these events. Three of these trailers could be hooked together and brought at the same time with one of Strang's innovative self-propelled cars doing all the work. This trailer is attached to the first self-propelled streetcar ever used on tracks, the *Ogerita*. (Overland Park Historical Society.)

IMAGES
*of America*

# OVERLAND PARK

Suzee SoldanEls Oberg and the
Overland Park Historical Society

ARCADIA
PUBLISHING

Published by Arcadia Publishing
Charleston, South Carolina


Library of Congress Control Number: 2012943460

For all general information, please contact Arcadia Publishing:
Telephone 843-853-2070
Fax 843-853-0044
E-mail sales@arcadiapublishing.com
For customer service and orders:
Toll-Free 1-888-313-2665

Visit us on the Internet at www.arcadiapublishing.com

*Dedicated to all the past and current members of the
Overland Park Historical Society, whose endeavors have
saved the history of the early city for future generations*

# CONTENTS

# ACKNOWLEDGMENTS

Suzee SoldanEls Oberg and the Overland Park Historical Society want to acknowledge the generous help and efforts of the many people who contributed photographs, information, and professional help in compiling this Overland Park history book. Through the years, many early residents and their descendants have generously contributed photographs and memorabilia to the society. Without those photographs and recorded memories, this book could not have been written.

Among those descendants are George Cox Jr., the Henderson-Hoffman family, Thomas C. Porter, Israel Breyfogle, and John Marty. Many residents of the 1930s, 1940s, and 1950s, like Andy Klein, Robert Jennings, Dr. Charles Abbott, Howard Docker, and Frank Schepers, have provided additional information and photographs about those decades.

The Blue Valley Historical Society donated artifacts, photographs, and assets when it disbanded. The Overland Park Heritage Foundation donated many photographs of early Overland Park buildings. The Heritage Foundation and Johnson County Heritage Trust Fund have been most generous in their financial grants to the Overland Park Historical Society, allowing the society to collect, preserve, display, and educate the community about the exceptional history of Overland Park and its surrounding area.

The City of Overland Park donated photographs of activities since incorporation in 1960. John Fowler devoted an enormous amount of time to examining and magnifying many old photographs for the preservation of Overland Park history. Florent W. Wagner, the society's historian and current president, without whom this book could not have been written, deserves an enormous amount of credit for the hours spent collecting photographs and answering the author's questions about them.

Unless otherwise noted, the photographs in this book were previously donated to the society or from the City of Overland Park's archives.

# INTRODUCTION

After Kansas became a state in the 1860s, the land where the Santa Fe, Oregon, and California Trials had crossed—and where Indians farmed and hunted while it was Shawnee Indian Territory—was eagerly sought by farmers who migrated west from other states. These pioneer families built homes, produced crops, bought stock, and settled down in this Kansas land that early explorers once referred to as "an uninhabitable desert." The fertile ground proved to be an ideal place for farms. Most of the township's farmland is now covered with homes and businesses. There are sketches and images of a few of the homes of those pioneer farmers, and, luckily, some of the homes still remain. Also, a few swales from the wagon trains that once traversed the area are still visible.

A flood in 1903 in Kansas City from the Kaw and Missouri Rivers led to the founding of Overland Park. The widowed mother of William B. Strang Jr. asked him to come and rescue her from the awful stench of rotting carcasses in the flooded stockyards that permeated the air of her home in Kansas City, Missouri. William, an international builder of short line railroads and with offices on Wall Street, resided at that time on fashionable Park Avenue in New York City.

In one version of this story, William, soon after he came to her rescue, took her to the farm of his friend, George Metcalf. It was several miles out in the country and across the state line in Kansas at what was then the intersection of Military Highway (now Metcalf Avenue) and Seventy-fifth Street. The rural postal designation for the farm area at the time was Glenn, Kansas. While she was staying there, she mentioned to her son how good the air smelled and how happy she was to get out of the city. As a result, the idea to build a carefully planned parklike suburb there, where the air was clean and there was no chance of flooding, was born.

With his railroading background, Strang's plan hinged on building an interurban rail line that would take commuters into the city from a place where a family could build an affordable home away from the urban grime and odors. The lots were to have space enough to keep a cow and chickens along with a garden. The breadwinner could enjoy a short trolley ride into Kansas City to his job. Strang planned a community where working people could enjoy a quality of life generally available only to the wealthy.

By 1905, construction of the interurban line was underway. Track was laid on high ridges close to the route of the Santa Fe Trail. Waiting stations along the route and a carbarn for maintenance were built. The *Ogerita*, named for Strang's niece, was the first car to arrive, in March 1906. It was luxurious for an interurban car, with a bathroom and the appearance of a drawing room. The innovative design of the electric self-propelled streetcar with no overhead wires was patented by Strang. It made news as it traveled from the East Coast to Overland Park with the Strangs, the engineer, and several dignitaries on board. It was the first self-propelled streetcar ever used on railroad tracks in the United States.

The streetcar was good advertising both for Strang's real estate venture and for the propulsion system that he wanted to demonstrate to other railroads. That design preceded the modern diesel engine used by railroads today. Two other cars followed within months, also named for family members. The interurban line was officially called the Missouri & Kansas Interurban Railroad but soon became known as the Strang Line to the public.

In 1906, Strang optioned his first 600 acres, which were advertised to be 126 feet higher than any other place in Kansas City, Missouri. The acreage that he named Overland Park reached from Seventy-ninth Street and Military Highway to Eighty-seventh Street and then west to Antioch Road. Strang's first marketing strategies included building a meeting hall and a baseball park, where potential customers could attend weekly dances and games.

An auction of Overland Park lots, held on August 28 and 29, 1906, resulted in the sale of 83 parcels, with the highest selling for the handsome sum of $380. As he acquired more land and planned additional developments, Strang's promotions became bigger and more varied. Roads were graded and businesses were built along the Strang Line on the new Santa Fe Avenue to accommodate residents and visitors.

In 1908, the spacious home Strang built for himself near the heart of his growing business district was finished and his wife, Margaret, was persuaded to join him. They had their seven carriages sent from New York, and a large wooden stable was erected for their horses. Strang also bought a Hupmobile limousine and had a sturdy, two-story limestone carriage house built, with living quarters above for his chauffeur's family and space below for his automobile and carriages.

Strang was fascinated by the idea of flight and arranged for a pilot to stop in Overland Park with his airplane on his way to California. Charles K. Hamilton, who had made a name for himself flying on the East Coast, arrived in Overland Park in 1909 with six cartons of parts and assembled his Curtiss biplane in a snowy field next to the interurban carbarn. The event was eagerly anticipated by the public, as most people had never seen a plane. The flight was contingent on late December's weather, so colored flags were hung on tall buildings in Kansas City to indicate the status of the flight. The exhibition flights began on Christmas Day and continued into January 1910. The interurban ran every 10 minutes during the scheduled flight times, bringing the public to Overland Park to see the takeoffs and landings.

By April 1911, Strang had constructed an airfield beside his Strang Line tracks at Eighty-second and Robinson Streets for pilots to use as a refueling stop on the way to either coast and as a place for the public to see flight demonstrations. By 1913, he moved his special dance floor from Santa Fe Hall to a new aviation pavilion with classrooms and a theater inside and with spotting towers on the roof. Crowds of 20,000 or more spectators attracted the air shows, circuses, and Wild West shows held there, giving Strang thousands of potential customers for his new community; his real estate agents mingled with the crowds at these events. He also built a lake in conjunction with the airfield, where families could enjoy fishing and swimming on weekends while staying in tents he provided.

In anticipation of World War I, the Army used Strang's airfield to teach combat maneuvers to young pilots who might be headed for the conflict. When the United States became involved in the war, Strang gave a pair of his favorite horses to the war effort. After the end of the war, as rock roads were completed to accommodate the growing use of automobiles, the Jefferson Highway and others like it made it possible for Strang's developments to expand farther away from the interurban line. Strang died in 1921, but the town he designed and named Overland Park in Mission Urban Township was firmly established by then. The downtown area had doubled in size.

In the 1920s, attending Overland Park School was so desirable that students rode the Strang Line from other districts to receive a superior education. As principal, Mabel Harrison was responsible for establishing a school system that became nationally recognized. Through the years, many families have chosen to live in Overland Park because of the schools. The high school, built in the 1920s, served several municipalities, including Overland Park, and was named Shawnee Mission Rural High School in reference to the local Methodist Indian mission that existed in the 1850s. The main post office that serves northeast Johnson County municipalities is also named Shawnee

Mission, and Overland Park residents and those in surrounding municipalities can receive mail with that designation as well as by their city's name.

The Great Depression kept Overland Park's growth to a minimum; however, in 1924, the Kansas City Power and Light Company moved its entire State of Kansas Division to a new building on the west side of Santa Fe Avenue between Seventy-ninth and Eightieth Streets. That industry and the surrounding dairy farms kept the economy of Overland Park relatively depression-resistant during those years. Unfortunately, the old Kansas City Power and Light Company building was lost to a large electrical fire a few years ago. It was owned by longtime downtown business owner Gil Rumsey and was used for his art gallery and an antique business. Fortunately, there are 12 buildings in the downtown area between 80 and 100 years old that have been preserved in remarkably good condition.

In February 1940, the Strang Line declared bankruptcy, although it continued running until July of that year. During World War II, patriotic citizens participated to help the war effort. The vacant right-of-way of the Strang line between Seventy-ninth and Eightieth Streets became a gathering place for scrap metal salvage. A previously closed lumberyard, in the business section on Eightieth Street, was used to manufacture wooden items for the military. Among the items produced were temporary wooden seats for female pilots to use when ferrying newly assembled planes from the Fairfax assembly plant to military bases for armament outfitting.

After World War II, developers like the Breyfogle Partnership built houses for returning soldiers. Their developments and the subdivisions of several other builders brought a huge increase in population and a lively economy. The old downtown was changed considerably. More modern retail spaces with offices above were constructed, and the small cottage that had once held the police department was torn down to make way for a city parking lot. The volunteer fire department, with its siren sending businessmen rushing out of their stores and scurrying into their firefighting gear, was replaced with a full-time department.

In 1960, the area of Mission Urban Township that had been designated Overland Park legally became a first-class city, the first time that a city was allowed this designation without going through the steps of third and second classes. Township officials maintained careful zoning laws and provided green spaces for citizens throughout the township's growth. Since incorporation, the city has been fortunate in its selection of elected officials. The mayors and city councils have maintained a superior staff and police department.

From 1967 on, big shopping centers and neighborhood strip malls have accommodated a large customer base from the entire metropolitan area. In 1973, Corporate Woods, a complex of high-rise office buildings in a wooded parklike setting, was begun, and national and international offices moved to the city, bringing thousands of employees. By the 1980s, national hotels and motels were built to accommodate visitors and large meetings.

In the 1980s, as outlying businesses drew customers away from the old downtown and the aging infrastructure there began showing wear and tear, business owners met and agreed to form a business improvement district. By taxing themselves and with additional financial input from the city, the old downtown was refurbished with streetscapes and a central Farmer's Market pavilion. The market and accompanying clock tower won an architectural award for designer Richard Coleman, then an employee in the city planning department.

In the summer months, concerts are held in the Farmer's Market pavilion on Saturdays, drawing big crowds. Historic old downtown Overland Park has also become popular with younger generations. Santa Fe Commons Park, near where Strang's home once stood, has a large bandstand where concerts are held each Sunday evening in the summer. Strang's old carriage house, in that park, was repaired and made habitable by the city. It is now the office of the Overland Park Historical Society. An annual juried arts and crafts festival is held each fall in the park in conjunction with a parade that draws tens of thousands of people.

Several important corporate headquarters are located in Overland Park, both in Corporate Woods and in their own complexes, such as Sprint's world headquarters on a 200-acre campus built to accommodate more than 14,000 employees.

On the 100th anniversary of Overland Park's founding, a seven-foot bronze statue of William B. Strang Jr. was installed and stands proudly on the corner of Santa Fe Avenue and Eightieth Streets, where the city began.

The city has expanded to include the communities of Stanley and Morse. The former Stanley State Bank's 1910 building at 151st Street and Metcalf Avenue was saved with the help of the city and the Overland Park Heritage Foundation and was relocated six blocks west to 151st and Newton Streets. In 1996, Morse Methodist Church, built in 1885, was saved and restored and is now used by another church.

Overland Park Convention Center, built in 2003, draws large crowds to conventions, trade shows, and performances. The expansion of Johnson County Community College and the amenities associated with it has brought it national acclaim. The Deanna Rose Children's Farmstead and the Overland Park Arboretum are also popular attractions. The latest addition to the city's recreational facilities is a 96-acre soccer complex, the only one of its kind in the United States.

The quality of life in Overland Park has been recognized by publications such as *Forbes* and *Money* magazines, as being among the Top 10 places to live in the United States. If he were alive to see how his city has excelled, William B. Strang Jr. would certainly approve.

# One

# IN THE OLD DAYS

This Lewis W. Breyfogle farm sketch is from the 1874 Johnson County Atlas. Lewis arrived with his father, Israel, in 1866, when the area became home to cattle, crops, and farmhouses. Most of those early houses are gone and exist only in old photographs and sketches. The families whose homes are on the following pages were important to the establishment of Overland Park.

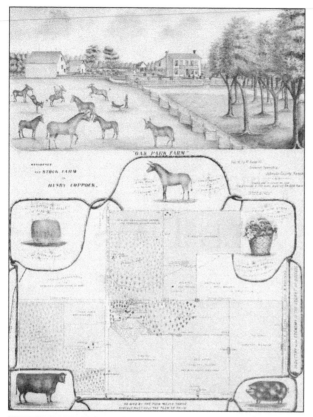

From the same 1874 atlas is the sketch (left) of Henry Coppock's 800-acre Oak Park Farm. The farm stretched from Seventy-first Street, on the south, to Sixty-third Street, on the north. Coppock came through Kansas in 1857 as a young man bent on adventure. After years of western travels, he returned in 1867 to Kansas and bought his huge holdings from Shawnee Indian chief Graham Rogers, who had lived there since 1828. Coppock's clapboard farmhouse was built by closing in Rogers's two existing primitive, two-story log cabins, connected by a dogtrot with fireplaces at each end. Believed to be one of the oldest structures in the area, it still exists inside the lovely home below, at Sixty-seventh and Mackey Streets.

The farmhouse of the Honorable Thomas James, seen in this 1874 sketch, was located close to 103rd and Glenwood Streets. In 1859, James brought his family to Kansas from Ohio. Growing crops and raising stock were difficult during the Civil War years, but his farm flourished afterwards, as did most others in the fertile Kansas soil. James acquired his honorary title for serving in the 1873 Kansas Legislature.

Andrew "Andy" James, the nephew of Thomas James, lived in this home, at 103rd and Glenwood Streets, which was remodeled from the 1880s farmhouse of William Perry Phillips. After acquiring the property in 1912, Andy sent for ship's carpenters from Boston for the project and used solid redwood for the columns. Andy raised purebred shorthorn cattle and was a well known auctioneer, conducting Overland Park real estate auctions in 1906.

The William P. and Margaret Bridges Goode farmhouse, a quarter mile west of Ninety-ninth Street and Metcalf Avenue, was built in the late 1870s. Four of the family's 10 children were born there. The senior Goodes and the first six children were born in Saline County, Missouri. A clay tennis court was added in the 1920s.

The Elijah Cornell Chase farmhouse, on Seventy-second Street at Antioch Road, was originally a wooden structure but had a brick addition in 1869. Elijah, a nephew of Ezra Cornell, the founder of Cornell University, came from New York in the 1850s to work at the Quaker Indian Mission a few miles north. When the Indians were sent to Oklahoma and sold their land, he bought 60 acres for this farm.

The 1873 Antioch Presbyterian Church was located at Seventy-fifth Street and Antioch Road. It closed in 1925. Quaker Missionaries first used the land for their Friends Meetings from the 1830s until they disbanded in 1871. The site now contains the Antioch Pioneer Cemetery, where many early settlers are buried and which contains a replica of the church constructed from the hand-hewn lumber of the old church and the original windows and pews.

The 1870s Corinth Presbyterian Church, at Eighty-third Street and Mission Road, and the Antioch Presbyterian Church, several miles away, shared a minister who traveled from the Westport area in Kansas City and alternated his ministry between the two churches. Only a small cemetery remains to indicate the site of the Corinth Church. In 1911, members and new town residents combined these churches and formed the Overland Park Presbyterian Church Society.

This substantial farm home of Louis D. Breyfogle Sr. was near Eighty-sixth Street and Metcalf Avenue. Louis was among the third generation of Breyfogle descendants to establish a farm near his relatives. The Breyfogle children are, from left to right, Mary, Hilma, Elmora, Louis D. Jr., and George Israel.

One of the oldest remaining farmhouses in the area is the Park House, at Eighty-seventh and Goodman Streets. A New England saltbox–style house, it was constructed about 1873 by David and Mary Park, who came from Pittsburgh. The porch was added later. Unfortunately, the Rocky Mountain Locust Plague, from 1874 to 1876, required David to leave for other work. Three days after he returned, he died.

Jacob and Electa Marty's farm was north of Seventy-fifth Street. The family migrated to Kansas about 1865. This photograph shows the Victorian farmhouse of their son John. Overland Park's Fire Station No. 1, the Marty Memorial Station, is located on this site today. John Marty was a leader in the new community and, in 1910, was one of the founders and a director of the new Overland Park State Bank.

Before rural free delivery, the Glenn Post Office, which served the area from 1868 until 1895, was located in the John Henderson family's farmhouse at Seventy-eight Street and Metcalf Avenue. After John's death in 1871, his widow, Sarah, and daughter Ida handled the mail, riding more than two miles on horseback to get it from the Merriam Post Office. The Andy Klein Pontiac dealership was built on this corner in 1951.

The Milburn-Foster house, built in the 1880s, is located at Sixty-seventh Street and Antioch Road. George Milburn retired to Kansas after owning the largest wagon company in the United States and bought the Coppock farm. Unfortunately, he was only able to enjoy life as a gentleman farmer for three years before he died. Today, Milburn Country Club occupies part of his land and nearby real estate developments bear his name.

Thomas Carson Porter and his wife, Ann, came to Kansas in 1858 and built this home about 1880 on the northwest corner of Seventy-first Street and Mission Road. They farmed there until they sold the land to a developer for a shopping center in 1928. Family descendants relocated to Ninety-first Street and Antioch Road, where they built a large dairy operation.

# Two

# RAILS TO SUBURBIA

In 1905, railroad builder William B. Strang Jr. acquired 600 acres of farmland on a ridge in Mission Township, Johnson County. He platted the land into large house lots where families could escape the grime, odors, and occasional floods of Kansas City. He named his development Overland Park and built an interurban railroad to bring customers to buy his lots and live in his suburb.

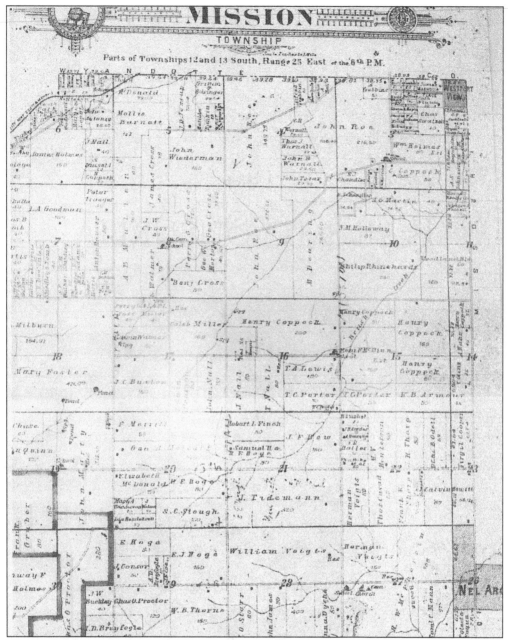

The land chosen by Strang for his new community is outlined on the left side of this map of the northern part of Mission Township, Johnson County. The township was named in remembrance of the several missions located in the county when it had been Indian Territory. The county was named for Rev. Thomas Johnson, who operated the Methodist mission from 1839 to 1862 as a manual training school for Indian children from the Shawnee, Delaware, and other tribes. Several buildings of the Shawnee Mission complex are preserved as a museum at Fifty-third Street and Mission Road in Fairway. The name Shawnee Mission was eventually adopted by both the area's school district and the central post office that services Overland Park.

Providing quick public access to his planned new community was a primary concern of Strang's. In 1905, he began the construction of his 20-mile Missouri & Kansas Interurban line from Kansas City, Missouri, to Olathe, Kansas. Mules and horses were used to grade the roadbed where oak ties were laid and 70-pound iron rails were spiked to them. The man on horseback on the right is thought to be Strang.

The interurban depot was constructed while the track was being laid and the streetcars were being built on the East Coast. The depot was beside the dirt track that had once been the Santa Fe Trail and at the intersection of what Strang would shortly have graded as Eightieth Street. As the development grew, the depot was enlarged.

In March 1906, the *Ogerita*, named for Strang's aunt, was the first streetcar to arrive for the new interurban line. The elegantly appointed interior even contained a bathroom. Its journey from the East Coast, with dignitaries on board, made national news because it was the first self-propelled electric car ever used in the United States. The patent for its design was only one of several railroad-related patents held by Strang.

Strang family members and handsomely attired visitors were enthralled with the *Ogerita*. The shiny, vermilion-colored streetcar and the newspaper accounts about it were wonderful advertising for Strang's interurban line. Strang used the publicity to his advantage to market both his new railroad cars and his developing real estate venture.

The *Marguerite*, named for Strang's wife, Margaret, was the second car to arrive from the East Coast, in August 1906. At 62 feet in length, it was a larger, more conventionally styled self-propelled car, with a muffler on the roof. Strang's self-propelled streetcars were the forerunners of modern diesel locomotives.

The interior of the *Marguerite*, although not as fancy as the *Ogerita*, was still comfortably designed for riders, with seats of plush printed fabric. The windows were curved to be aesthetically pleasing and there were decorative electric light fixtures on the ceiling. It also had a bathroom and a smoking section for patrons' convenience.

As novel and plush as the *Marguerite* was as a streetcar, it was used as a freight car by 1915. This farmer loads his produce as the *Marguerite* is stopped on the tracks across Eightieth Street. Strang pioneered the freighting of less-than-carload lots, allowing local farmers to ship to Kansas City and other more distant markets without waiting to accumulate a carload.

By the Fourth of July in 1906, the interurban transported these city dwellers and local farm families to Overland Park to take part in the dances and parties held in Strang's new Santa Fe Trail Hall. Inside was a maple dance floor, installed over a frame and resting on springs, which was a hit with dancers. The hall was a successful marketing ploy, luring customers to Strang's real estate venture.

After his streetcars were in service and available to transport customers, Strang ran this advertisement in the *Kansas City Star* newspaper on August 25, 1906. It is one of two full pages showing ample platted house lots, graded streets, and the Santa Fe Trail route of his interurban line. The line's track was laid to avoid any future flooding problems. The advertisement extolls the delights awaiting customers who built homes there and lived in the suburban area he had named Overland Park. Clean air and space for a garden, a chicken house, and a cow are emphasized. Free natural gas was offered, as was free transportation to the upcoming two-day auction of homesites on August 28 and 29. Buyers had to abide by several restrictions regulating the price and size of any house they intended to build; Strang demanded quality in his new suburb.

A celebration of the arrival of the self-propelled *Geraldine* was held in the spring of 1907. The streetcar was named for a niece of the Strangs. William B. Strang Jr. is seen on the far left with his brother, Robert, on his right. Invited dignitaries are posed around the motorman, who is third from the right in his cap and goggles.

The *Irene* was the last of Strang's self-propelled streetcars to arrive. Made of steel, it was the finest of the four cars, and it proudly advertised his company on the side. It was named for his sister's young daughter, Irene Catherine Kennefick, who married Charles Vernon Jones in 1909. Jones was the son of one of the founders of the Jones Store Company in Kansas City.

This photograph shows the inside of the *Irene*, which had the most elegant interior of the four cars. Casually placed along the sides were cushioned wicker chairs, with plush drapes on the windows and carpeting on the floor. Fancy globe electric lights on the ceiling provided illumination. The interior resembled a drawing room of the period. The *Irene* and the *Ogerita* were in service for less than two years before Marion Willis Savage, the owner of a railroad line in Minnesota, bought them in 1908. Savage used the fancy self-propelled streetcars to transport visitors to his Minnesota ranch to see his horse, the legendary harness racer Dan Patch, who lived from 1896 until 1916 and was the most famous horse in America at the time, attracting many admirers. Even now, a historical society devoted to him displays artifacts relating to the remarkable stallion's life.

In 1906, Strang built a native limestone, 6,000-square-foot carbarn to service and maintain his interurban electric streetcars. This photograph shows the carbarn with the 2,400 square feet he later added to house electric generators. In the background is the 60-foot wooden water tower he built for his new town. It has since been replaced with a metal water tower that proudly displays the Overland Park logo.

By 1908, the self-propelled streetcars were converted to use overhead electric lines. Two 50,000-watt Buckeye Electricity generators were installed in the enlarged carbarn to run the converted electric cars. The generators ran on natural gas piped in from wells located on Strang's original 600 acres. Seen here in the foreground are Tom Linn (left) and Leo Davis, two of the several electrical engineers employed in the building.

After Strang's self-propelled streetcars were modified to run on electricity, several second-generation cars were put into service on the line. The numbered cars were then designated as trolleys for the interurban line, commonly referred to as the Strang Line. In this photograph, members of the extended Strang family pose in front of the Overland Park depot and real estate office with the youngsters waving out of the windows of trolley No. 102. In 1906, a local chapter of the Daughters of the American Revolution placed the stone marker in the foreground to mark the Santa Fe Trail. In the 1980s, the marker was rededicated by the DAR, and it can now be found three blocks west of Metcalf Avenue on Eightieth Street, just east of Santa Fe Avenue.

Thomas Riley was employed by Strang as the general manager of both his interurban line and the Strang Land Company. Riley was sometimes referred to as Strang's "right hand." Riley Street in Overland Park is named for him. Many Overland Park streets are named for other Strang employees, business owners, and early settlers, like Metcalf Avenue and Marty Street.

Bill George also held an important job in the Strang operation. Strang hired him to head the crew that maintained the many miles of roadbed for the interurban line. George and the members of his crew made their homes in several small houses located beside the carbarn.

# *Three*

# ABRACADABRA AND
# IT'S A TOWN

This Strang Line patron waits for a ride in front of the depot, which included the real estate office at the time. In that office, Strang planned the layout of his town, carefully molding the town to his liking and finding the best locations for new businesses to be constructed so they could accommodate new residents.

Strang had 5,000 new trees shipped in and planted along the newly graded streets in his development. He also wanted green spaces to enhance the appearance of Overland Park's new business area. A new building is in the background. Strang's brother Robert is on the left in one of the seven carriages Strang shipped by rail from New York City.

In 1907, Overland Park's first restaurant was built to cater to the crowds of visitors. The wooden structure was located north of the Santa Fe Trail Hall and east of the tracks. According to stories about the early building, a dining table was permanently reserved for Strang. The structure survived into the 1930s.

The town is seen here in 1906, before the first run of the interurban. The Santa Fe Trail Hall, built for the entertainment of potential lot purchasers, was placed on the old Santa Fe Trail road between rows of existing trees. Trees lined the road, which had previously led to the C.O. Proctor farmhouse. On the left, the first commercial building is under construction.

This newly constructed 1906 commercial building at the northwest corner of the Santa Fe Trail and Eightieth Street held several business entities. There were four businesses in the front part of the building: a grocery store, a tobacco shop, a confectionery, and the Strang Land Company office. A side door accessed a barbershop located in the back. O.B. Carver, the proprietor of the grocery store, stands in the doorway.

By 1911, Strang's Overland Park development had modern electric streetlights rather than gaslights. Strang's land office, on the right in this photograph of downtown, had moved back to the Strang Line depot and no longer shared a space in the building on Santa Fe Avenue. Strang added a bandstand in the center of town for the musical entertainment of his potential customers on the weekends.

This crowd in front of the Santa Fe Trail Hall is believed to have been gathered for a baseball game in Overland Park. The games were advertised in local newspapers and drew competing teams from towns as far away as Lawrence. The young man in the foreground wears a baseball glove. The new Mills and Linn houses are in the background.

In 1907, Grant Conser built a wood-frame building at Foster and Eightieth Streets and moved his general store there from its previous location at Seventy-ninth Street and Metcalf Avenue. When the wooden structure burned in August 1910, he replaced it with this two-story brick building. The first floor was used for his mercantile store, and the second floor had apartments and a large meeting hall.

This odd early building was referred to as the "flatiron building" because it had a flat roof and was on a triangular lot resembling the shape of an iron. The *Overland Park Herald* was published out of this building in the late 1920s. A Standard Oil service station owned by George Cox was built on this site in the 1950s.

In early 1910, this stucco building on the southwest corner of Foster and Eightieth Streets was in the process of being built by Asa M. Wood, a former farmer and dairyman, to house his fledgling insurance and real estate business. The Overland Park Post Office opened in the northwest corner of the building that same year.

After the first commercial building burned in 1911, it was replaced with the Voigts Building in the footprint of that structure. This photograph from around 1915 shows the grocery store, soda shop, and pharmacy on the first floor. Professional offices and apartments occupied the second floor. It burned again on Armistice Day, November 11, 1927. The one-story building that replaced it is now used as law offices.

Earl Turner owned this barbershop, with two barber poles, on Santa Fe Avenue. According to a 1922 article in the *Olathe Mirror* written by the editor, John W. Breyfogle, Turner gave a very good shave without an undue wait. Turner and his wife, Stella, owned a substantial home on Seventy-ninth Street between Marty Street and Overland Park Drive. He was also the manager of the Overland Park baseball team.

In 1917, this building, owned by Grant Conser, was converted from a barbershop to an ice plant. His son, Albert, stands in front of the business. On the left side of the building are the gasoline engine and muffler used to compress the gas to freeze 300-pound blocks of ice.

While his own home was being built, Strang lived in this house constructed by Charles O. Proctor, who was a farmer in Mission Township as early as 1895. A high-rise apartment building is now located on the original homesite on Santa Fe Trail Drive between Eightieth and Eighty-first Streets. In 1906, the house was moved to the southeast corner of Eightieth and Marty Streets, where this photograph was taken that same year.

After it was finished in 1907, the new Strang home, on Eightieth Street east of Overland Park Drive, was a gathering place for friends and family, as seen in this photograph. Strang's wife, her niece, and his brother, Bob, all lived there, but guests and relatives were also encouraged to visit. Strang was particularly proud of the concrete public sidewalks and graded streets in his town.

Margaret Strang's contemporaries considered her to be a charming beauty. She was born in Ohio to G.W. and Sarah Morrison in 1868. A Morrison family legend says that William B. Strang Jr. first saw her in Oklahoma Territory, where her father was working. Strang was there building a short line for the Atchison, Topeka & Santa Fe Railway and was smitten when she appeared from behind a mound astride a white horse. The couple married in Wellington, Kansas, and made their home on Park Avenue in New York City before 1902. Margaret was reluctant to leave the social life and cultural advantages of New York, but, in 1908, she was persuaded to move to the new home that her husband had built for her in Overland Park. Her brother, George Riley Morrison, lived nearby with his large family.

This view looks southwest from Seventy-ninth Street and shows platted, improved land with new suburban homes in the background in 1910. To comply with Strang's cost restrictions, the houses were on half-acre or acre lots with room for a small barn for the family cow. Many of the barns became garages when automobiles became popular.

In 1910, the Hodges Brothers Lumber Company of Olathe opened a branch lumberyard at Eighty-second Street and Newton Avenue. In the 1920s, the lumberyard moved to Seventy-ninth Street and Santa Fe Avenue and the old location became the Mission Township garage and yards. Later, the original site became the pole yard for Kansas City Power & Light Company.

This photograph of a mule team and wagon on Overland Park Drive shows the Armstrong house in the background. The handsome home, built in 1912, had a dance floor on the third level. The minimum cost requirement for any house in the subdivision was $2,500, but the Armstrong house was built at the hefty cost of $6,000. The original Overland Park Presbyterian Church is on the right.

About 1909, Tom and Sophie Linn built this home on Seventy-ninth Street about half a block from the carbarn where Tom was employed as an electrical engineer for the interurban. Tom was well known and was a sought-after contractor for homes for new residents in his spare time. The Linn daughters, Mildred and Marjorie, enjoyed growing up in this Victorian house.

The Leonidas "Lon" Cave house (above) was on the southeast corner of Seventy-ninth Street and Overland Park Drive. It was ordered out of the 1908 Sears, Roebuck and Co. catalog and was constructed of machine-made concrete blocks shipped to Overland Park on the railroad. Lon Cave, seen in uniform at left, was a conductor on the Strang Line when the house was built. He only worked for the line for two years, after which he was elected Johnson County sheriff, serving from 1910 until 1913. In 1914, he bought the Keyser Hardware Store on Santa Fe Avenue.

This pretty two-story bungalow, built about 1910, was on the east side of Overland Park Drive between Seventy-ninth and Eightieth Streets. John Mills, a retired firefighter from Kansas City, lived there with his wife, Edna, and their children, Lela and Claude. John helped the new town by offering his experience and expertise in firefighting.

When Grant Conser's building burned in 1911, Conser's Enterprise Telephone Company moved to this house on Eightieth Street, across from the bank. It is believed that Enterprise was sold to the Home Telephone Company, whose office and switchboard operated here until the early 1950s. The Home Telephone Company eventually became part of the Southwestern Bell system. In 1954, the house was moved to Eighty-fifth Street and Metcalf Avenue.

The first bank building in the district was the Overland Park State Bank, east of the depot on Eightieth Street. The bank was chartered in 1910 and opened for business on March 3, using the depot until its building was completed in 1911. At the dedication, ladies were given fans and gentlemen were given cigars. Prosperous local farmers, including John Marty, C.A. Pincomb, John Pettyjohn, John Hyde, J.D. New, F.D. Cross, E.E. Voigts, Willard James, L.D. Breyfogle, and Frank Hodges, were on the first board of directors, along with William B. Strang. So many people wanted stock in the new bank that some people had to be left out. The bank moved into a new building in the 1950s. Cosmopolitan International now owns the old, beautifully preserved structure, using it as its international headquarters.

The headquarters depot for the Strang Line was enlarged in 1910 and landscaped with plantings and trees by the fall of 1911. The whitewashed tree trunks prevented sunscald of the tree bark from the bright winter sunshine, and the matching painted trolley poles and telephone poles added to the parklike setting of the business district. Strang wanted his development to include green space and trees with a spacious appearance to live up to the name Overland Park. The newly opened Overland Park State Bank building is in the background on the right, and the Overland Park Restaurant is in the background on the left. Park benches were provided for patrons near the depot and in the surrounding grassy area.

The Strangs (above) were photographed in their fringe-topped surrey drawn by Strang's prized pair of horses, Old Bob and Black Beauty, in 1915. During World War I, Strang wrote a letter to Gen. John J. Pershing stating that since he had no son to send to war, he would send his two favorite horses instead. Unfortunately, Black Beauty died in South Carolina shortly after being separated from her mate. Below, in November 1918, Lt. Col. Ruby D. Garrett of the 117th Signal Corps Battalion, 42nd Division, was photographed in camp astride Old Bob after the armistice in Berlin. The 42nd Division was known as the Rainbow Division after Maj. Douglas MacArthur stated that the volunteers, who hailed from 26 states and the District of Columbia, were so diverse that they would stretch over the country like a rainbow.

This structure, built after 1910 by John Knox, was used primarily as a feed barn to provide grain and hay for livestock on the new larger dairy farms now surrounding the town. E.M. Coleman and J.H. Baker were the proprietors of the business, which also sold chicken feed for the growing home chicken and egg industry.

Strang constructed a large private stable to house his horses that he had shipped to Overland Park from New York City. The stable was on Santa Fe Avenue north of the new business buildings in the background. This photograph was taken looking south across Seventy-ninth Street, with Foster Street on the right.

This bird's-eye view of the new town was taken in late September 1911. The view looks south from the water tower beside the carbarn. Strang spared no expense in hiring a professional photographer, a Mr. Williams, to photograph the new community with a camera that used the new panoramic technology. Seen prominently on the left side are Tom Riley's house and the John Mills house.

In the center is Strang's stable, between Santa Fe Avenue and Foster Street. The Grant Conser house and other new residences are on the right. In the left background are the Nicholson house, the Strang house, and the new bank building, with the business district in the center.

William B. Strang Jr. (left) and his brother Robert take a break from work in the depot office to pose for this photograph. Robert served as the company comptroller. William's marketing strategies pulled in thousands of people on the weekends by providing quality family entertainment. He constructed a lake, with tents for family camping. In 1908, when the interurban was changed into an electrically operated trolley system, electricity was made available for schools and churches, which was another big draw for customers looking for a better place to live. Strang was also enthralled with the flying feats of the Wright Brothers. In 1909, he arranged for a flight to occur in Overland Park, the first in the area, and subsequently built an airfield for air shows.

# *Four*

# FIRST TRAINS, THEN PLANES AND AUTOMOBILES

The trolley *Ogerita* is seen here with some of the 20,000–25,000 people that came to events in Overland Park disembarking from it. The Strang Line was quite popular with Kansas City families, who were able to catch the trolley to Overland Park from Eighth and Main Streets, where a ticket office was maintained. Olathe patrons could catch the northbound trolley from the south side of the courthouse square.

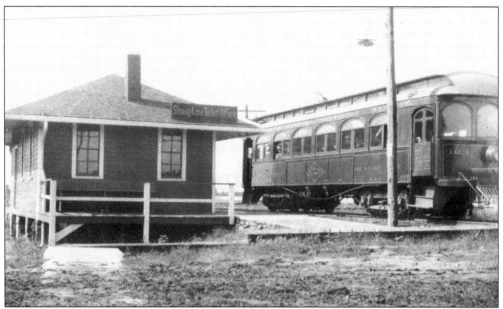

The Lenexa depot, built in 1906, was a full-service depot for ticket purchasing and freight delivery. It was located on the south side of the St. Louis-San Francisco Railway (Frisco) tracks, west of Pflumm Road. The Strang Line had a siding there—provided by the Frisco—that allowed freight cars to be diverted to the line for delivery anywhere along the route, from the city market in Kansas City to Olathe.

Strang provided waiting stations along the interurban line near churches and schools for the comfort and convenience of customers, like at the Southridge station, seen here, which was near the Southridge School and Southridge Presbyterian Church, east of Fifty-first Street and Roe Avenue, where he developed a subdivision in 1908 in what is now Roeland Park.

These photographs show the first airplane flight in Kansas. Strang arranged for a daring young aviator, Charles K. Hamilton, who was on his way to California, to stop in Overland Park with his Curtiss aeroplane to demonstrate flying. Most people had only read about flying in newspapers. The plane was shipped by train in six cartons and assembled on the snow-packed Overland Park baseball field near the interurban carbarn. The flight was scheduled to occur on December 25, 1909, weather permitting. Widespread interest in the event was at a fever pitch, and colored flags in downtown Kansas City were hung on buildings to alert the public as to the flight status. When red flags—indicating flight—appeared, there was a rush to the scene. Several other demonstration flights followed in January 1910.

The 1909 ball field at Seventy-ninth Street and Santa Fe Avenue, with the covered grandstand that Strang had built for Overland Park baseball matches, was subsequently used as the first airfield for demonstration flights. The field was an ideal size since planes only needed 150 to 200 feet to take off and land. The hanger in the background was built for pilots to use while at the field.

When there was a shortage of aviators with motorized planes, Strang used gliders that were stored in tents on one side of the field to entertain people in the grandstand. One motorized plane towed a glider skyward, and the glider would then circle around the field for as long as 15 minutes, much to the delight of the crowd.

DeLloyd "Dutch" Thompson was nationally known as a daring early aviator. He evidently had a problem taking off here at the Overland Park field. The plane was taxiing across the field and is believed to have had a wheel fall into a hole causing it to flip up on its nose. According to reports, the propeller was only slightly damaged.

After repairs to the propeller, Thompson was able to successfully take off and show his skill. He was one of the pioneers in aviation who perfected the "loop-de-loop." The daring aerobics he put his aircraft through were spectacular. Thompson remained a respected authority on flight and aircraft throughout his life.

This aerial photograph was taken in 1914 looking north toward the town from around Eighty-seventh Street. Gliders are shown circling above Strang's new Aviation Park and field. On the right side is Strang's man-made South Killarney Lake, with the camping tents used for overnight stays. The Irish name he used for the lake reflected his Irish heritage. Both his mother, Catherine Fleming,

and his father, William B. Strang Sr., were Irish immigrants. On the far left in the background are the pavilion building and the grandstands, where weekend patrons watched baseball games on Sunday mornings and aviation activities on Sunday afternoons. The lake is now called South Lake and is located between Robinson and Riley Streets on Eighty-seventh Street.

# South Killarney Lake

## Fishing Season is Now Open

### For a Vacation that Bristles with Recreation and Fun go to

## Overland Park

Dancing,

Hay Rides,

Camping,

Aeroplaning,

Canoeing,

Fishing

Your Vacati
This Year

Make it one c
tinuous round
healthful, rest
pleasure by spe
ing it at Overla
Park, the pl
ground of Kan
City. Here d
moments are
known. Everyo
boys, girls, wom
men, all enter i
the spirit of h
piness, conte
ment, pleasure a
health, breathed
this beautiful, w
derful mount
resort. A vacat
spent in the hi
lands of Overl
is one long to
remembered.

## The Strang Electric Line

### The Most Beautiful Scenic Ride Out of Kansas City

Thos. Riley, Manager

This advertisement from a Kansas City newspaper lists all the recreational opportunities available for visitors to South Killarney Lake. Strang provided canoes and had the lake stocked with fish. The writer of the copy for this advertisement compares the experience to a mountain vacation. For only 50¢ per person, a family could ride the interurban to Overland Park and then rent a tent at the lake where they could spend the night after a day of watching air shows or a musical show in the pavilion. Tents could be rented for longer stays. Days were spent fishing, canoeing, and relaxing in the high-country atmosphere of Overland Park. Evenings were spent dancing on the pavilion's special dance floor.

A future hot air balloon race gave Strang the opportunity for an exhibition of balloons on the Overland Park airfield. Scheduled to ascend was a balloon by the name of *Kansas City III*, which was to be flown in an upcoming race by European aviator Moritz Bozarth. Balloon rides were offered, but the main event was an exhibition of fancy and trick flying by Robert Fowler and Thornwell Andrews, flying in Wright and Curtiss biplanes. This took place in July 1911, and Andrews returned for an exhibition in September. The advertisement for these Overland Park events also lists all the reasons for building a home there. Strang used every opportunity to market his development and placed his agents among the enthusiastic crowds to encourage real estate sales.

In September 1913, Strang moved the maple-spring dance floor from the former Santa Fe Trail Hall to this large pavilion, where he also provided a stage and storage for scenery backdrops. Classrooms and offices for an aviation school were on the south end. Spotting towers above the roof and large windows that rose into the ceiling for summer ventilation were other features. A veranda surrounded three sides of the building.

In 1913, a mock battle was held at Fort Leavenworth between the "Blue Army" from Fort Smith, Arkansas, and the "Red Army" from Fort Riley, Kansas. As a promotion, Strang arranged to have them bivouacked on Overland Park land, and they spread their tents at South Killarney Lake. While there, the infantry and the cavalry paraded for the public. Their horses were picketed along the east side of the park.

This Wright Brothers Model B airplane was a pusher style. The interested public inspects the plane at the Overland Park airfield in 1912. Planes of that era were constructed of very lightweight materials such as lacquered silk or cotton muslin stretched over bamboo or a similar material for the wings. Because of this, they required constant maintenance—they also cost as much as a nice house.

The two-seater airplane in this photograph was made by the Bristol Aeroplane Company of the United Kingdom. These planes were used by the military in World War I for reconnaissance and fighting. When it ran out of fuel and made a forced landing in an Overland Park farm field near Seventy-ninth Street and Metcalf Avenue, a neighbor ran out with a camera and took this photograph.

In 1914, thousands of people watched the weekend shows in Overland Park's Aviation Park at Eighty-first Street and Santa Fe Avenue. The first airfield of its kind in the Midwest, it hosted air shows, circuses, Buffalo Bill's Wild West Show, and numerous other entertainments. Aviators particularly liked the field's south winds, which provided a lift for the wings of their aircraft. On the left is one of five grandstands spread around the field. At left center is the south side of the

pavilion building. Leaning against the pole in the center, William B. Strang stands with military observers. Although the Wright Brothers never came to Overland Park, many of their planes were flown here. At right is a Wright Brothers plane with uniformed military personnel nearby. Many Army Air Corps pilots were trained to fly at this field.

Strang's chauffeur, Vance Edgar, poses in 1914 beside Strang's limousine. Edgar, his wife, Myrtle, and their son Thomas Leroy lived in Strang's large carriage house at 8045 Santa Fe Avenue, where this automobile and several carriages were kept. By 1915, as automobiles became increasingly popular with local residents, Strang would boast that there were more than 20 miles of rocked roads in the town.

Even though rocked roads were better than getting stuck in the mud after a rain, the roads in use in the early days of motoring were hard on tires. Leo Davis converted Strang's personal stable into a Dreadnaught Tire store, where he sold the popular 1910s brand and did automotive repairs.

Fuel for early vehicles was available from the gas pumps seen on the right at the Santa Fe Garage. The Breyfogles constructed this building, which was originally a hardware store owned by Frank Keyser. Lon Cave bought it and then sold it to Frank Schepers, who is standing in the doorway in this image. Later, it was converted to a bar and grill and has passed through several owners.

About 1921, Grant Conser built this building on the west side of Santa Fe Avenue near Eightieth Street for his Acme Garage and Machine Works. His son, Albert, stands on the far right. The location had been the site of the public stable. In later years, it became the bus station and, recently, it has been an automobile paint and supply store.

In 1922, Frank Schepers (squatting on the right) constructed this garage over Strang's private wooden stable on Santa Fe Avenue. Schepers repaired automobiles and operated a Buick dealership. In 1923, the volunteer fire department held a fundraiser here, netting $70 for the Community Boys Band. Later, this space was used by the Kansas City Power and Light Company to maintain its vehicles and store supplies.

A Ford Model T truck, like the one seen here, was converted to a community fire truck by the addition of two 50-gallon chemical water tanks, a hose, ladders, and tools by Frank Schepers, Herman Lee, Roscoe Campbell, and George Cox. It was kept behind Schepers' garage. Cox became the first chief of the volunteer fire department.

By 1928, Metcalf Avenue, used as Highway 69, was improved south of 151st Street with the addition of six inches of concrete with brick on top. Three men carried the bricks to champion bricklayer "Indian Jim," James Cleveland Brown, who was able to lay more than 1,000 bricks per hour. This road was originally the 1830s Military Road leading to Fort Leavenworth from forts in the South and East.

This marker, placed at Eightieth Street and Metcalf Avenue, designated the National Old Trails Road from New York to Los Angeles. When the Kansas route of the Jefferson Highway, America's first transcontinental international highway—from Canada to New Orleans—was selected, it crossed here. By 1927, named highways with their colored route stripes on telephone poles became obsolete, as the US government began the numbering system.

Strang was enthralled by moving photographs, establishing the Overland Park Movie Company and envisioning Overland Park as the movie capital of America. The subject matter of these movies was likely to include trains, planes, or automobiles since motor-driven vehicles greatly interested him. None of his films have been found, and they are believed to have been thrown away. The name of Strang's movie photographer, seen here, is not known.

Near the end of his life, Strang's funds were tied up in real estate. While he was said to be "land poor," he was proud of the 100 buildings existing in Overland Park by 1920. He did not live to see the Kansas division of the Kansas City Power and Light Company relocate to Overland Park in 1924. The company's office is seen here in this 1935 photograph looking south on Santa Fe Avenue.

## *Five*

# TRANSITIONS

Willliam B. Strang
Jr. died at the Elms
Hotel in Excelsior
Springs, Missouri,
where he had gone
for the medicinal
springs, in 1921. His
wife ordered this
mausoleum and sold
the airfield pavilion
to pay for it. Only
after her death, six
years later, when both
of them were moved
from a Kansas City
cemetery to Lenexa
Catholic Cemetery,
was the beautiful
marble mausoleum
used for their remains.

This handsome 18-year-old Overland Park native is Cpl. Dwight J. Cowles, who was killed in World War I and was buried on July 15, 1918, at Fort Leavenworth. His parents, Leonard and Emma Cowles, bought the airfield pavilion from Margaret Strang, turning the building into a feed mill. The American Legion Dwight Cowles Overland Park Post 370 was chartered in 1923 and named in his honor. The post used a small house called "The Hut" at Seventy-ninth and Foster Streets until 1954, when this building, shown below under construction at 7500 West 75th Street, was constructed. A large parking lot is shared by the fire station on the west side and a swimming pool in the northwest corner of the block.

Seen here in the 1920s are the 76 employees of the Kansas City Power and Light Company who worked out of the Overland Park office on Santa Fe Avenue. Some of their names are printed along the bottom of the photograph. Most of these employees made their homes in the town and raised their families in Overland Park, which meant more houses were built, more businesses were started, and the schools had more attendance.

Kansas City Power and Light Company linemen pose in front of one of their trucks, which they nicknamed "Big Brutus." It had to live up to its name and be tough to travel the back roads where line work was often needed. The men also had to be tough and strong to climb the poles and lift the equipment.

A mobile kitchen was used to demonstrate and sell electric appliances to customers at county fairs and other events. The marketing of these appliances was profitable both because the sales and because of the increased electricity they used. When the electric company was challenged by appliance retailers, the state passed a law preventing these sales and the marketing strategy was abandoned.

By the early 1950s, with the growth of its maintenance area, the Kansas City Power and Light Company was in need of more space for the storage and maintenance of its equipment. The company leased the empty carbarn and remodeled it for its purposes. The Highway 58 signage indicates the route where it went through downtown Overland Park, using Seventy-ninth Street and Santa Fe Avenue.

The John D. New dairy farm was at Ninety-fifth Street and Metcalf Avenue. In 1955, Glen Dickinson bought the property for a motel and theater location. On the right is the barn that he used for many years as the Manor Barn Restaurant and Dance Hall.

These two men, Herbert Ford Sr. (left) and Hal Stonebraker, were responsible for the design and construction of many new buildings in the town. Ford brought several years of contracting experience with him when he moved to Overland Park in the 1920s, and Stonebraker was a talented architect and a 1920s graduate of Kansas University.

The Wood brothers bought Maple Crest Farm in 1920. It was located north of Seventy-ninth Street from Nall Avenue to Glenwood Street. Their milk trucks made morning deliveries with a stop at the Waldo Ice Plant in the afternoon, where they were filled with ice for overnight cooling use at the dairy. When the brothers purchased a 1930s electric cooler, it paid for itself in one year.

This herd of Holstein, Guernsey, and Jersey milking cows was photographed in the pasture of Maple Crest Farm. The 100-acre dairy farm was one of the largest in the area. New housing developments can be seen in the upper left. Overland Park's dairy industry helped the area economically during the hard times of the 1920s and 1930s.

In the image above, brothers Frank (far left) and Kirk Wood (far right) pose with the milking men at their dairy. The Wood brothers were the sons of A.M. Wood, a successful Overland Park businessman. The dairy had 10 delivery trucks (below) in the 1920s and 1930s. The drivers, who made daily household deliveries in both Kansas and Missouri, stand beside their respective trucks. It is believed that this dairy serviced the largest number of home delivery routes in the area.

In the 1930s, the Wood brothers acquired a one-third partnership in the Country Club Dairy in Kansas City. The dairy purchased the Holmes Guernsey Farm at Eighty-fifth Street and Antioch Road and created the Country Club Dairy's Show Farm for public tours. The milking barn is seen above. The image below shows the separation of cow breeds, with black-and-white Holsteins on the right. The Holsteins were high in production, but their milk was low in butterfat. The Guernseys and Jerseys, on the left, produced less milk in volume, but it was very high in butterfat. The milk was blended together to make premium white-listed milk with 3.2 percent butterfat. The excess butterfat was then used to make ice cream. Today, the Greenbrier Townhouses and Apartments are on the former farm.

These 1930s photographs show Porter Brothers Dairy, the longest-surviving Overland Park dairy with home delivery. The Porter brothers, Audley and Earl, operated the farm, west of Antioch Road, which consisted of 40 acres on the north side of Ninety-first Street and 80 acres on the south side. In addition, they rented hundreds of acres in surrounding fields to raise feed for their cows. Below are their two barns, which date from 1933. In the image below, the barn on the right was used for milking the cows, one of which was a prizewinning Holstein that produced a record 14 gallons of milk per day. The barn on the left was used for bottling and packaging the milk products after homogenization. The barns were used until the business was sold in 1952.

This aerial view of the Porter Brothers Dairy shows the extent of the dairy farm in 1933. Antioch Road is on the right, and Ninety-first Street cuts through the middle of the farm. The operation used agricultural methods taught at Kansas State University, in Manhattan. The modern 1930s guidelines it used included terraced pastures, which was a first for local dairy farms.

Earl Porter purchased this handsome country bungalow in the 1940s, and it is still owned by the Porter family. At Ninety-first and Farley Streets, it was to the west of the Porter farm. It was originally built by the Moody family around 1910. Strang Park, a neighborhood park, is just north of the home today.

In 1941, Hugh White purchased the Wolverine Dairy, between Eighty-fifth and Eighty-seventh Streets on the east side of Metcalf Avenue. Hugh, seen here with his wife, Mary, and their truck, operated the dairy with the help of their four children until 1949. The two eldest children, Bob and Louise, helped deliver the milk. Louise also helped her mother prepare food for the hired hands.

When Wolverine closed, the auction of its stock and equipment brought an enormous crowd of bidders. Once the equipment was cleared from the property, in 1950, the White family turned the land into a real estate development they named White Haven Estates. Several homes were built for family members, and lots were sold to other builders.

Edith and Fred Roy came to Overland Park in 1919 and rented a farm at Eightieth Street and Metcalf Avenue. In 1920, they purchased five acres between Seventy-ninth Street and Eightieth Streets on Roy Street (now Hardy Street), where they operated a small dairy. Fred was a teacher of industrial arts in Kansas City, and he served on the Overland Park school board for many years. (Courtesy of Debbie Roy.)

The four Roy children are seen below. They are, from left to right, Walter, Elaine, Charles, and Robert. After serving in World War II, Walter and Robert owned Roy Brothers Construction in Overland Park, building many homes for veterans like themselves. Elaine worked in Kansas City as a school nurse, and Charles worked for the United States Department of Agriculture for many years. (Courtesy of Debbie Roy.)

In September 1909, the new Overland Park School opened on land donated by Strang at Eighty-second and Procter (now Lowell) Streets. It accommodated grades one through eight in two schoolrooms, with space in the basement for assemblies and a gymnasium with adjacent locker rooms. In the 1913–1914 school year, there were 78 students and two teachers. By 1916, an addition was added to the north for a high school.

On January 11, 1920, an overnight fire at the school devastated the community. Rebuilding started immediately for a planned three-story brick school with four rooms for the elementary grades on the main floor and four rooms on the second floor for the high school. The ground floor had a gymnasium, locker rooms, and space for assemblies.

The Overland Park grade school children, displaced by the fire, attended school in the basement of the Baptist Church at Eightieth and Conser Streets. The school district provided funds to electrify the building. The high school students attended school in the Conser Building on the second floor. The new school building was ready by the fall term.

In 1930, the Overland Park teachers are, from left to right, (first row) Ms. Stevenson, Mrs. Gorsage, Miss Perdue, and Miss Vance; (second row) Mrs. Stone, Miss Vickers, Mabel Harrison—the principal for 38 years—and Beatrice Perdue; (third row) Miss Sublett, Miss Wood, Mr. Hall, Miss Brown, and Ms. Miller.

The Strang Line's management pioneered freight pickup and delivery for farms and homes using 1920s Ford pickup trucks. This innovative service kept the Strang Line in business during the depression years of the late 1920s and 1930s. The service continued until shortly after the line's last passenger run in 1940.

After a 1925 fire in the Overland Park carbarn, this third-generation electric trolley car was used on the Strang Line. It is seen here at Roanoke Parkway and Thirty-ninth Street in Kansas City. The signage at the top of the car reads, "Mo. & Kan. R.R. Co."

When the Voigts Building burned in 1927, the fire also consumed the dental office of Dr. Charles A. Abbott. When Dr. Abbott was asked to be chief of the volunteer fire department, he insisted that a new truck be purchased. He is seen here in that new 1920s truck. Abbott served as chief from 1927 until he went into the service during World War II.

Overland Park Fire Department volunteers often rushed to a fire from their homes or businesses at the sound of the siren from the fire station on Foster Street. Members of the department are seen here in front of the Overland Park School, where they had gone to show the children the town's new 1930s truck. Included in this photograph, among the rest of the department, are Chief Charles Abbott, Leo Davis, and Frank Schepers.

By late 1940, the railroad crossing sign seen above on Santa Fe Avenue at Seventy-ninth Street was no longer needed. Automobiles, trucks, and the Depression made the bankrupt Strang Line run for the last time. The rights-of-way and other assets were sold. During World War II, when scrap metal and other materials were needed for the war effort, they were accumulated where the track had been. In the photograph below, taken on one of the line's last runs, Tom Riley, the general manager of the line, stands on the left, and John Schwartz, the freight manager, is in the cab of the *Marguerite*.

John Barkley (left) was a Medal of Honor recipient in World War I. Overland Park's Barkley Street was named for the family's dairy farm, where John and his wife, Marguerite Marie Mullen Barkley, lived after he returned from the war. The photograph below was taken at a 1970s Overland Park Kiwanis Club meeting. Bob Jennings (left), a civic leader and the owner of Jennings Lawn and Garden, shakes hands with Barkley, who worked in the Overland Park area for many years and participated in community organizations. In retirement, among his other good works, he was instrumental in working towards the completion of Antioch Park, at Sixty-fifth Street and Antioch Road, and Shawnee Mission Park, on Renner Road at Seventy-ninth Street.

# Six
# ALL GOOD SPORTS

J.W. Stoker, a National Cowboy Hall of Fame inductee, has won many honors for his proficiency at riding and roping. The young Overland Park schoolboy signed with a manager at age 10 and traveled the world performing. He has impressed millions with his talent as a stunt-double in movies and in his numerous television appearances.

Young J.W. Stoker (right) and his friend Holland Harpool learned to ride in an Overland Park club founded by Harpool's father, Henry. Stoker became so proficient at trick roping that, at age 12, he appeared on a Wheaties box as the Juvenile World Champion trick rider.

The Santa Fe Trail Riders was made up of Overland Park youngsters who took part in rodeo competitions in surrounding states in the 1930s. The group, with more than three dozen riders ages 6 through 18, won prizes wherever it appeared. Members practiced east of the carbarn and west of Sixty-fifth Street and Santa Fe Avenue in a farm field.

The Mission Valley Hunt Club had members from Overland Park and the surrounding area. They hunted wolves and coyotes while riding across farm fields from the Missouri-Kansas state line in the east to Kansas City Road leading to Olathe in the west. Joe Mackey, who was also active in the Mission Brook Polo Club, was the hunt master.

The polo club used the Ralph Nafziger farm at Eighty-seventh Street and Mission Road for its practice field and for matches. The hunt club required only one horse per member, while polo club members needed three or four horses. This photograph shows the intensity of the matches. The field is now a park at Eighty-seventh Street and Roe Avenue.

In 1943, Segner Field was the fourth and final baseball field Chris Segner built. It was located at Eighty-seventh and Grant Streets. After the end of World War II, the Kansas City Power and Light Company installed lights, making it possible to play night games. The field was a popular addition to the area.

The Segner team was sponsored by the grocery store owned by Emma Segner. This team photograph was made in the 1940s. Other local businesses and organizations, like Andy Klein Pontiac and the American Legion, also sponsored teams. After her husband's death, Emma continued to manage the field until 1955, when it was taken over by the Three and Two Baseball Club. In 1962, the games were moved to new fields farther west.

A Scottish theme and bagpipers helped celebrate the formal dedication (above) of the existing St. Andrews Golf Course, on 135th Street near Switzer Street, when the city acquired it and made it a public course. Both St. Andrews and the Sykes/Lady Overland Park Golf Club, at 125th Street and Quivira Road, are operated by the city and are among the most popular courses in the metropolitan area because of their affordability, playability, design, and amenities. The St. Andrews course offers 18 tree-lined holes, and the Sykes/Lady course offers 27 regulation holes and a nine-hole par-three course. Both courses are affiliated with local, regional, and national golf associations. The players below have a nice view of the city.

Christie Ambrosi, a player on the American softball team in the 2000 Olympic Games in Sydney, Australia, holds her Olympic gold medal. She attended high school at Blue Valley Northwest High School in Overland Park and went on to UCLA, where she was an All-American all four years and played on the team that won the NCAA Division I National Championship.

The Marty swimming pool at Seventy-fourth and Conser Streets was initially a private pool operated by a corporation that sold memberships to residents. Its popularity led to its having a waiting list in the 1960s and 1970s. These youngsters on the Overland Park Swim Club, posing here in 1975, practiced before it opened for the day. They competed with other teams in the metropolitan area. (Courtesy of Robbie McClure Kearney.)

After the Marty pool was purchased by the city, several other pools were built and maintained for residents. The redesigned pool above now features a children's slide through the mouth of a frog. The outdoor pool at Tomahawk Ridge Community Center is seen below. The center, at 119th Street and Lowell Avenue, is one of two community centers for area citizens. On the northeast corner of the property is the Korean War Veterans Memorial, which has the names of fallen heroes inscribed on a wall. A bronze statue of a mourning soldier is in the patio area.

Matt Ross opened a Ben Franklin Store in 1949 at Eightieth Street and Santa Fe Avenue. He quickly became a civic leader and was elected to the Mission Urban Township board in the early 1950s. He was also elected to the first Overland Park City Council when the city incorporated. Ross participated in many community activities and served on the police board, the zoning commission, and the zoning appeals board. After his retirement, he worked at the Overland Park State Bank, where he was an officer and a member of the board. When names were suggested for a new community center downtown on Floyd Street at Eighty-first Street, Ross's name headed the list.

## Seven

# THE REST OF THE STORY

The Dragon Inn Restaurant now occupies the historic Conser Building at Eightieth and Foster Streets. The restaurant has been in business in the downtown for more than 40 years. The Kot family also operated an Asian grocery store for a few years in the 1940s in the fire station building north of the restaurant on Foster Street. Their restoration of the Conser Building preserved the architectural elements of the 1911 structure.

The business climate downtown changed dramatically in the 1950s. By the end of the decade, on Metcalf Avenue (Highway 69) south of Seventy-fifth Street, there were numerous automobile dealers and two new motels. Offices and retail spaces were built in the downtown area, replacing the houses of earlier times. Among the retailers were four dress shops, two shoe stores, three children's stores, a fabric store, beauty salons, a furniture store, two dime stores, grocery stores, a department store, a men's clothing store, barbershops, and many places to eat, including the fountains in the several drugstores. Hardware stores sold household goods and sports equipment as well as automobile supplies and hardware. Customers could find any kind of service and buy anything they needed downtown. They could also catch a bus connecting to anywhere in the United States at the Overland Park terminal.

In the late 1940s and early 1950s, Glen Dickinson's new Overland Theater in the business district was used for Sunday services by the newly formed Overland Park Christian Church until its church at Seventy-fifth and Conser Streets was finished. Some of the church members are seen above. In the summer months, the church held outdoors services on Sunday mornings at the New 50 Hiway Drive-In movie theater near Santa Fe Avenue and Eighty-seventh Street (Highway 50). Below, Rev. Forest Haggard preaches from the roof of the concession stand; he could be heard through the car speakers. The choir and the ushers stand below him. When used as a church, it was the second-largest drive-in church in America, second only to one in Hollywood.

There were many church denominations in Overland Park, including St Mark's Methodist Church (above), at Sixty-fifth Street on Santa Fe Avenue on the old Strang Line route. This photograph was taken on Easter Sunday 1951. The church had previously been at Sixty-fourth and Floyd Streets in the 1920s. The 1930s Overland Park Presbyterian Church (below), at 8029 Overland Park Drive, is shown with Boy Scouts holding a flag ceremony in the 1950s. The church was enlarged after World War II and has been known throughout its more-than-100-year history for the availability of its buildings for community purposes outside the scope of religion. It has served as headquarters for the Northeast Johnson County Welfare Chest and the Shawnee Mission Red Cross. Since the 1960s, it has been the office and distribution point for Shawnee Mission Meals on Wheels. (Above, courtesy of Peggy Lee; below, courtesy of Overland Park Presbyterian Church.)

In 1957, after they sold their dairy and completed their housing development, the Hugh White family built the attractive White Haven Motor Lodge on Metcalf Avenue at Eighty-first Street, which became a landmark. They used diamond-paned lead glass windows and had beautifully decorated rooms. For more than 50 years, the family-operated business was known for extraordinary service; its sign seldom showed vacancy.

Overland Park contractors started Suburb Decorations at Santa Fe Avenue and Eightieth Street in 1954 to supply materials for the enormous number of houses being built. The business began inside the stone-and-wood Strang Line depot, which was covered with a brick veneer and had an extension to its west side. The Oetting family has operated the business from the beginning and is now into its third generation of family ownership.

The still active Overland Park Masonic Lodge No. 436, on Overland Park Drive at Eighty-first Street, occupies the original stone building constructed by the Overland Park Presbyterian Church in 1913. The cornerstone from the church was taken out in 1930 and replaced by the lodge's own cornerstone indicating its founding date of 1923.

Charles Fatino completed this two-story building at Eightieth and Floyd Streets in 1958. Retail spaces held businesses like the Joe and John Davis family's Trail Gift Shop, the Davis Liquor Store, Suzee's Fashions, Erma's Children's Shop, and Herman's Beauty Salon. Offices were upstairs, and the popular John Francis Overland Restaurant, on the west side of the building, supplied meeting rooms and drew customers from a wide area for more than 30 years.

Some businesses have endured through several generations in downtown Overland Park. Above, Ellis Witter and his son Jerry stand in front of the 1930s Witter Plumbing and Electric building at 7514 West Eightieth Street. The elder Witter started in the plumbing business in 1928, buying the establishment in 1938. He was an active, generous member of many organizations. Jerry Witter still owns and operates the business today. Below, on February 14, 1958, Dorothy Soldanels and her daughter Suzee pose in front of their new women's clothing store, Suzee's, at 7140 West Eightieth Street. The store was in business for 53 years, 42 of them in downtown Overland Park. Suzee's daughter, Robbie McClure, also worked in the business for several years, and all three women participated in business associations and were active in civic clubs.

When Overland Park incorporated as a first-class city on May 20, 1960, the municipality continued to use the Mission Urban Township offices on the second floor of this 1920s building on Eightieth Street, which was owned by Walter Fleming. The city offices occupied space previously used by the civil engineering firm of Shafer, Kline, and Warren. The police department was on the north side of the building, and there were administrative offices on the south side. Below the offices on the same block were popular businesses like Corwin's Dress Shop and Bauman's Shoe Store. Mary and Everet Corwin of Corwin's and Maxine and Lee Bauman of Bauman's were active community leaders.

The city quickly outgrew the facilities in Fleming's building and moved a block south to a new structure at Eighty-first and Marty Streets. The city administrative offices and the council room, which was used for meetings and as a judicial chamber, were on the main floor. The police department occupied the lower level and had a portable iron jail for temporarily holding prisoners.

In 1967, the city offices moved into a new, larger city hall on vacant ground that was once part of the Holmes Guernsey Farm. The top level is used for public works, community development, and other offices. The council chamber and offices, including those for the mayor, city manager, and city clerk, are on the main floor. The building has been enlarged several times.

Prior to incorporation, a Mission Urban Township law required the establishment of a police department for the Overland Park area. This little house located between Seventy-ninth and Eightieth Streets on Marty Streets was one of two structures that served as police department and courtroom in the 1950s. At the time, the police staff was minimal.

In the early 1970s, a much larger police force required a building separate from the city hall. The department's building was constructed across the street at 8500 Antioch Road. Initially, it held courtrooms, staff offices, and temporary jail cells. A large parking lot housed an ever-expanding number of police cars and employees. The building's name has been changed from the Overland Park Police Department to the Myron E. Scafe Building.

Myron E. Scafe served as chief of the Overland Park Police Department for 24 years. He started in 1954, before the city was incorporated, when the department was still run by Mission Urban Township. As chief, he guided the enormous growth of the department. Ben Casteel and John Kenyon were chiefs before Scafe, and John Douglas followed him.

When the growth of the city required additional space for the police department, the construction of the W. Jack Sanders Justice Center at 124th and Foster Streets was the city's answer to the problem. The chief's office and other administrative offices, along with the municipal court, are located there. The center was named for the longtime city council and police commission member.

The city has been a leader in acquiring the newest firefighting equipment available. The importance of having extension ladders was dictated by the building of high-rise office and apartment buildings. The trucks are received at the fire-training center at 125th Street and Antioch Road. The center is also used for training by other municipalities. The fire stations all accommodate these trucks and other emergency vehicles.

James G. Broockerd, who joined the department in 1950, followed Howard Docker as fire chief, being elected to the role in 1956. He was with the Overland Park Fire Department for 31 years. The station at Ninety-fifth and Grant Streets is named for him. The department's growth has followed that of the city, and there are now five strategically placed stations.

This historic bungalow on Seventy-ninth Street between Floyd and Marty Streets is now painted a pretty blue color and houses a dog-grooming business. The 1910 building was originally the Bishop family home but has been used for business purposes for many years. One couple that owned it was in the clock repair business and added the unusual big clock hands above the door, with the working parts in the attic.

The Metcalf Bank, at Seventy-ninth Street and Metcalf Avenue, was the second bank to open in Overland Park. It was started by Kansas City banker Joseph Cohen in the 1960s. Ben Craig became president in 1964, keeping that post for almost 50 years. He continues with the bank today as chairman emeritus and has been a leader in the community and participated in many civic clubs and activities through the years.

A tornado described as a "white tornado" struck Overland Park on the afternoon of April 19, 1966, just as schoolchildren were being released from classes. It came down out of a clear blue sky, with no prior warning, and hit the roof of the Katherine Carpenter Elementary School at 9700 West Ninety-sixth Street. Children were rushed back into the shelter of the school by the principal, and no one was injured. After it hit the school roof, it went on northeast and hit neighboring homes, which were damaged or, in some cases, completely destroyed. Afterwards, the trees were littered with insulation, rugs, toilet tissue, boards, and other debris. Fortunately, the tornado lifted back into the clouds and did no further damage in the city.

In the mid-1970s, a children's farmstead was proposed to the city and, in 1976, a children's petting zoo (above) became a reality at 137th and Switzer Streets. In the early 1980s, Overland Park police officer Deanna Rose (right) was killed in the line of duty, and in 1985, the farmstead was renamed in her honor. The popularity of this tourist attraction has grown with several additions, including an American Indian tribal council lodge and some buildings that are representative of an early-20th-century farming community. More than half a million people visit the attraction annually.

In 1990, television star, producer, and director Michael Landon (second from left) brought his film production company to Overland Park to make the television movie *Where Pigeons Go to Die*. The front half of a house and other scenery was constructed on Ninety-fifth Street just west of Metcalf Avenue. The film, about raising racing pigeons in the 1950s, features Art Carney. Landon died the next year at age 55.

When the Glenwood Theatre and Glen Dickinson's large motel at Ninety-first Street and Metcalf Avenue were torn down to make room for a strip mall, the Mossman brothers, experts at theater restoration, rescued this sign and Dickinson's plush, comfortable theater seating. They installed the sign in the parking lot of Metcalf South Shopping Center and the seats inside the center in their own theaters.

This hybrid electric car was received by the City of Overland Park after the city made an effort to be more environmentally conscious. Mayor Ed Eilert stands beside the car. Eilert served as mayor for 24 years, during which time the city became the second-largest in Kansas. He carefully guided the city financially and helped it achieve and maintain a AAA credit rating.

The Overland Park Lions Club was organized in the late 1950s. In the 1960s, it started displaying American flags along Metcalf Avenue for important national holidays. The "Avenue of Flags" has become a traditional treat for motorists. Through the years, other organizations have assisted in the installation of the flags from Seventy-fifth Street south to approximately 123rd Street.

The 300-acre Overland Park Arboretum and Botanical Gardens was started in the early 1990s. The official dedication of the Erikson Water Garden is seen above. On the left, greeting visitors and dignitaries, is Don Pipes, Overland Park's city manager for 34 years. Many benches, trees, and gardens throughout the park have been placed or created through donations on behalf of family members. The park is constantly growing and changing as an educational, cultural, and recreational resource for the region. A future garden has been proposed featuring a train with a replica of old downtown Overland Park in the center. Below is the Environmental Education Visitors Center, which showcases innovative and practical environmental building features and technology.

The Blue Valley School District 229, primarily located in Overland Park, was created in 1965 as part the unified school district. Blue Valley Northwest High School, seen here, is one of the district's five high schools. Students are drawn from 20 elementary and nine middle schools south of Interstate 435. The district recently had more than 18,000 students.

Facilities at the Kansas University Edwards Campus, at 126th Street and Quivira Road, include the Regents Center and Regnier Hall. Students can receive degrees from Kansas University in Lawrence after attending college at this campus in Overland Park. Continuing education is also available. Modern buildings with all sizes of meeting rooms and state-of-the-art equipment are offered to businesses and other educational groups at a nominal fee.

This band is from Shawnee Mission West High School, at Eighty-fifth Street and Antioch Road. In 1993–1994, the band was selected for a trip to London and invited to participate in a Christmas parade. West belongs to school district 512, which consists of 34 elementary schools, five middle schools, and five high schools. Three of the five high schools are in Overland Park, including Shawnee Mission West, Shawnee Mission South, and Shawnee Mission North, the original rural high school. Nationally known graduates of these high schools include former chairman of the joint chiefs of staff Gen. Richard Meyers, actors Paul Rudd and Jason Sudeikis, and television personality Phillip Calvin McGraw, commonly known as Dr. Phil.

Johnson County Community College was created at the behest of county voters in 1967. The first buildings were finished in 1972, and the college has expanded dramatically since then and now includes the renowned Nerman Museum of Contemporary Art. Works of art are also scattered throughout the corridors in several college buildings. The college, on College Boulevard at Quivira Road, has grown to have one of the largest undergraduate enrollments in the state of Kansas. Degrees and certificates are offered in a wide range of fields from business and web technologies to nursing and railroad operations. The school's Carlsen Center arranges a performing arts series and shows in three theaters that are well attended by the community. The aerial view below shows how much the campus has grown.

In the 1990s, the Sprint World Headquarters Campus was built on 200 acres in Overland Park. It was planned to accommodate more than 14,000 employees in one location. As the largest brick project in the world, it has been referred to as a "city of brick." The grounds include native grasses, a lake, and exercise trails. The massive campus has a main eastern entrance on Nall Avenue at 117th Street.

Corporate Woods, an award-winning office park in an imposing landscape, stretches from Antioch Road to Overland Parkway and from Interstate 435 to College Boulevard. Since the 1975 opening, many Fortune 500 companies have located there due to the desirable quality of life in the area. Many festivals are held there for charity and attended by thousands, including the Fourth of July celebration organized by the Overland Park Rotary Club.

Overland Park's first foray into shopping malls was the building of the French Market, with a concept of individually owned departments under one roof. Built at Ninety-fifth Street and Metcalf Avenue in 1962, it only lasted for five years. In 1967, a banker/owner built a large shopping center, Metcalf South, across the street, with major department stores anchoring each end of the two-block-long building. Oak Park Mall, the second major shopping center built in Overland Park, is seen below. A few miles west at Ninety-fifth Street and Quivira Road, it is the largest in the entire metropolitan area and draws customers from other states.

The Overland Park skyline is seen here from College Boulevard, west of Metcalf Avenue, in this image showing the city lights at night. In 100 years, the view changed from farmland to this. The lighting of homes and buildings also went from natural gas to electricity. College Boulevard

is on the left, and 110th Street is on the right. Executive Hills buildings are on the left, with the Overland Park Marriott Hotel and the Lighton Building—with its lighted pyramid on the top—behind. In the foreground are shopping centers and other business buildings.

In 1985, as the city grew south, the Stanley area, on Metcalf Avenue at 151st Street, was annexed. When the historic Stanley Bank needed to be moved to make room for a street improvement, it was donated to the Overland Park Heritage Foundation, which relocated it six blocks west. The Overland Park Historical Society assisted in the creation of a historic display inside, including a commemoration of the great Oxford vote fraud of 1857.

This old photograph of Morse Village, now part of Overland Park, looks northeast, with Quivira Road on the right and 155th Street at the top. The John Fifield country estate is on the lower right side. Morse was founded in 1885 as a stop between Kansas City and Springfield on the Kansas City, Clinton & Springfield Railroad. The Morse area was annexed along with Stanley in 1985.

The 1930s photograph above shows the Morse Village railroad depot. Across the tracks is the Morse grain elevator. The depot was used by the Kansas City, Clinton & Springfield Railroad, commonly known in the community as the "Leaky Roof Railroad" because some of its old freight cars were too leaky to hold grain. Those leaky cars were only used for other freight that moisture would not damage. The railroad was used by commuters to Kansas City. The Bank of Morse is seen below in the 1920s. The 1910 building has been well maintained through the years and is now a residential property.

Antioch Acres is one of many pocket parks created for residential neighborhoods and maintained by the parks department. This park is located on Hardy Street south of Seventy-second Terrace. These neighborhood parks carry forward William B. Strang Jr.'s idea of having green space for residents to enjoy. Overland Park is a designated Tree City USA and has a forestry department.

This photograph was taken in the 1990s and shows street improvements in the older, northern part of Overland Park. The city public works department is responsible for building, updating, and maintaining infrastructure. Over the years, it has been known for speedy snow removal in the winter and for keeping the streets clean and repaired.

The city holds an annual Arts and Crafts Fall Festival in Santa Fe Commons Park, on Santa Fe Avenue west of Eightieth Street, on the same day that a fall parade winds through the streets of downtown. Thousands of shoppers come to purchase unusual items and to enjoy the food vendors and the musical entertainment provided on the bandstand. The land for the park was purchased in the 1980s by the city and now contains public restrooms, a bandstand, a gazebo, bronze artworks, tables and benches, and walking paths leading to a bricked patio beside the Strang Carriage House. The bandstand is used every Sunday evening during the summer months, when the city provides band concerts and other musical entertainment in the park. Patrons are encouraged to bring blankets or lawn chairs and enjoy the free concerts.

The annual downtown fall parade has been held, rain or shine, for more than 50 years. The entries range from high school bands to Scout troops and usually number more than 100. Thousands of onlookers line the route, which follows the old Santa Fe Trail west on Seventy-ninth Street and then south on Santa Fe Avenue to Eighty-first Street.

The St. Patrick's Day parade was an annual Downtown Overland Park Business Association event in the 1980s and 1990s. It was started by the Holy family, the owners of Overland Interiors, which was located at that time in the old Voigts Building on Santa Fe Avenue. The Overland Park Jaycees were also active in promoting and helping with the event, which raised money for the Muscular Dystrophy Association.

For several years, an annual
nighttime holiday parade with
decorated, brightly lit floats has
wound through the streets of
old downtown. A tree-lighting
ceremony underneath the clock
tower is timed to coincide
with the arrival of the float
holding Santa Claus. Children
are invited to visit Santa for
a photograph and a treat.

Concerned downtown business
owners agreed to tax themselves
to acquire infrastructure updates
and beautify the aging area,
forming a business improvement
district in the 1990s. Some of
the results were streetscapes,
downtown's landmark clock
tower, and the Farmer's Market
pavilion. The city did its
part in the funding and has
since formed the Downtown
Overland Park Partnership to
continue maintaining the area.

In the early 1980s, the Downtown Overland Park Business Association started a farmer's market in a parking lot on Marty Street between Seventy-ninth and Eightieth Streets. Local growers were encouraged to sell their produce out of the backs of their trucks or off collapsible umbrella tables. The market's initial success led to the construction of a covered market pavilion on that lot, between Marty Street and Overland Park Drive. During the growing season, customers crowd the market on Wednesdays and Saturdays, buying locally grown produce and enjoying musical entertainment under the clock tower on Saturdays. Vendors from all around the area also offer food choices. The city now manages the market, which draws customers by the hundreds.

Strang's Carriage House in Santa Fe Commons Park, at 8045 Santa Fe Avenue, was restored in 1985. It was used as a shelter house until the 1990s, when it was refurbished for the Overland Park Historical Society's use as an office and for displaying artifacts and exhibits. The society's goals are to preserve artifacts and historic buildings, to establish a museum, and to educate the public about Overland Park's history.

On the 100th anniversary of the founding of Overland Park, the Overland Park Heritage Foundation, the City of Overland Park, and the Johnson County Heritage Trust Fund, with the assistance of the Overland Park Historical Society, held a celebration for the installation of a seven-foot bronze statue of founder William B. Strang Jr. at the intersection of Santa Fe Avenue and Eightieth Street, where it all began.

Visit us at
arcadiapublishing.com

......................................................